Oh, Lord, I Sound Just Like MAMA

Lynne Alpern and Esther Blumenfeld

Illustrated by Paulette Livers Lambert

Peachtree Publishers, Ltd.

Published by
PEACHTREE PUBLISHERS, LTD.
494 Armour Circle, N.E.
Atlanta, Georgia 30324

Manufactured in the United States of America

1st printing

Library of Congress Catalog Number 86-60009

ISBN 0-931948-93-2

*To my mother, Ruth, for a lifetime of laughter, and with
loving memories of my mother-in-law, Sarah*

. . . Lynne

To my mama, Ruth, and my mama-in-law, Fannie

. . . Esther

*For their sound advice — given, heard, remembered,
and appreciated . . . but rarely taken.*

Contents

"If I had known when you were growing up, that you were going to remember everything I did with total recall, I would have been more careful."
—Phyllis Walker

Preface

"Aim high and settle." Hardly a shocking bit of advice, but when we heard a friend talking about her mother's words of wisdom, Lynne's immediate reaction was to remark that a mother would never advise her son to compromise *his* goals in life. Why a daughter? By the end of our lunch the conversation became full of memories of what we women recalled hearing from mother on various topics. Some of this advice came straight from the mouth of Benjamin Franklin; some reeked of guilt. Many words were humorous because they were so outdated and frankly provincial, geared to an old-fashioned lifestyle.

Mothers' words of wisdom still have an impact on modern women. Certainly this relationship has been rediscovered in today's literature, and countless serious books analyze the complexity of the mother-daughter bond. But where are the laughs?

By the next morning the memories of our lunchtime conversation had sparked the idea for this book, an entertaining collection of colorful advice, sayings and criticism women recall hearing from their mothers and grandmothers. We set up our office — a table at a local McDonald's — and were on our way. Soon we became accepted regulars there, gaining a reputation as those two eccentrics who needed four hours and six tables for two cups of coffee. We knew we had it made when the manager began taking phone messages for us.

Our method of collection was hardly scientific. We did, however, want information from a cross section of women who varied in age, background and geographic location. We therefore interviewed by phone and mail; spoke and listened at women's groups, businesses and national conventions; interviewed celebrities; placed notices in publications across the country; and appeared on radio talk shows.

Our first radio program fell on Labor Day, an obvious but unintentional coincidence. Three minutes before show time the host arrived, clamped earphones on our heads and mikes around our necks. We jumped in cold, clammy and wary. The first caller told us her mother had ruined her life, and on this cheery note we began.

Amazingly, however, the response from most females — from nursery school youngsters to senior citizens — was similar. Initially, "Mother didn't tell me anything," or, "I really can't remember," followed in a few minutes by an outpouring of sayings and homilies. Many came directly from *Poor Richard's Almanac*. But some, like "Go with the creep to meet the crop," were unique, and these were the ones we wanted. Our questions prompted strange, poignant, funny and sometimes downright awful responses from women eager to share their memories with us.

We were surprised to find out what is remembered from the endless stream of advice mothers impart to their daughters. Selective memory is capricious, and we would defy any mother to predict what her daughter's recollections would be.

Through generations mothers have inspired, guided, supported and encouraged; or insulated, intimidated, discouraged and overwhelmed their daughters with suggestions or criticism. And although we do not want to repeat our mothers' mistakes, we are unconsciously bound by her example. Thus daughters frequently bewail, "Oh, Lord, I sound just like Mama."

The results of Mama's advice, sometimes misguided, are revealed in the anecdotes throughout the book. All are true. Many concern our own mothers and grandmothers or others who brightened our lives with warmth and humor. It is safe for us to laugh at our own mothers, because they have to forgive us. We did, however, promise not to tell the story of Aunt Emily and the hanging.

The chapter concerning prominent women is of special interest to us. Perhaps, we thought, the secret of their success would be revealed in the advice they received from the important women in their lives. Instead we discovered that these outstanding women had mothers and grandmothers much like the rest of us. No great revelation of the secret of success but perhaps something better. By their gracious sharing of remembered words of wisdom, they allow us to touch them in a special and personal way.

If you experience a twinge of recognition while reading this book, you share the feelings of most of the women who contributed material to it. At times it is akin to the sweet remembered taste of ice cream eaten off a flat wooden spoon, but at other times it more resembles the dull throbbing of a toothache.

The purpose of this book, however, is not to analyze but to entertain. Perhaps in the course of reading these pages, you too will recall some advice from your mother. We would enjoy your sharing it with us.

Here, then, for your reading is a non-exhaustive compendium of the advice hundreds of women remembered. Of course, it would never have been written had mothers only realized that their daughters were fully grown by the age of six.

Lynne Shapiro Alpern
Esther Richter Blumenfeld
Atlanta, Georgia

"You have to call your book *On Deaf Ears*, because that is where all the advice falls."
— Ruth Miller Shapiro

"As soon as you get your first book published, you must begin on your second, because you cannot live on past glory."
— Ruth May Richter

Dating And Men

Go With The Creep
To Meet The Crop

When I was a little girl, my beautiful Aunt Ruth had many boyfriends. It was my misfortune to fall madly in love with the one who owned a convertible. Often, when he came to call, he would take me for a ride around the block before going out with Aunt Ruth.

One evening, overcome with jealousy, I shut myself in my room and sobbed, because I knew that I could never compete with Aunt Ruth. I was also filled with remorse because I loved her dearly. Apparently overhearing the crying, she came into my room, sat on my bed, and said, "Honey, I'll make a deal with you. I'll play with him until you grow up, and then if you want him you can have him."

I have long since forgotten the man but must admit that once in a while I still get a pang for that car.

—E.B.

When they first met face to face, it should have been back to back.

*

If he wants you to cure his pimples, tell him to go to a dermatologist.

*

Is there anything you'd like for me to tell you about sex? If so, ask your sister.

*

Keep a hatpin in your lapel in case you have to stick it to him.

*

When you see a man go for his fly, you fly.

*

Cross your legs, and use your elbow.

*

Him you should kiss only on the forehead.

*

It's just as easy to do something wrong early in the evening as late at night.

*

If he tells you he loves you, it's just because his glands are active.

*

If it's important, ask him after he's eaten.

*

It's more important to be good in math than in history, because Catherine the Great won't keep you from getting pregnant.

*

Never kiss a man on the neck. It does terrible things to him.

Mother had attended football games fairly regularly since she was ten and thought she knew as much about the game as most women. Whatever I knew about it, I learned from her. One day my father was discussing a line-up with the family, remarking that the Oilers had a fine quarterback.

"Who are the other quarterbacks?" Mother asked.

"What other quarterbacks?" Dad countered, looking surprised.

"There are four, aren't there? One fullback, two halfbacks, and four quarterbacks."

No wonder the jocks never asked me out!

—L.A.

Keep your legs together, your pants up and stay in a room with a crowd.

*

Don't swim in the same pool with boys because sperm can float.

*

Well, at least his ears are close to his head.

*

You can leave your heart in San Francisco, but bring your virtue home.

*

If you don't know what to do when a boy gets fresh, say the Hail Mary.

*

Don't read *True Romances*; you'll end up pregnant.

*

When I asked your grandma about sex, her answer was always, "Shh, don't ask me. I don't know."

All men are alike; they're just looking for one thing...the right size knothole.

*

So what if he's short? Walk on your knees and enjoy yourself.

*

The only affair I ever had was catered.

*

Sex will age you if you enjoy it.

*

Be nice to the shmoe. Today's square may become tomorrow's success.

*

You only have a curfew if you are dating someone we don't like.

*

I think you should know sex might be kind of messy.

*

So what if he's younger than you are. Who's counting his teeth?

*

Sex. It happens but smart girls don't talk about it.

*

Only double date in a car with a couple you can turn around and talk to.

*

Never let a man answer the phone. It'll break your father's heart.

*

A forty-five-year-old man who still lives with his mother will make a lousy husband.

If you want to get rid of that pesty boy, invite him over and we'll fix squid.

In Israel when you walk down the street, remember that ninety-five percent of the boys are Jewish.

*

If he likes sports, you be his athletic supporter.

*

You must be a good girl if you want to wind up happy and successful and vacationing in Florida.

*

Honey, there isn't nothing in this world wrong with sleeping with someone. It's what people do when they ain't sleeping that creates all the commotion.

*

When it comes to your sexual encounters, spare me the blow-by-blows.

*

When you are out on a date, just think what Jesus would do.

*

If you're going to live together, why don't you just get married? We'll pay for the divorce.

*

It's a man's world? So let him think so.

*

Grandma never told me about sex. But when I played kick-the-can, I learned all kinds of secrets from the knowledgeable person I was hiding with.

*

A man's conscience is behind his zipper.

When I am asked how I met my husband, I explain that he has a meddling aunt who arranged our first date. Aunt DeVera is the only person in the world as stubborn as Warren.

When he protested that he was devoutly opposed to blind dates, she countered with, "All you have to do is take her out. You don't have to marry the girl."

So he married me out of spite.

Boy, did he get even with *her*.

—E.B.

Learn the difference between a warm heart and hot pants.

*

Don't let your good vibes activate his vibrator.

*

A girl can run faster with her dress up than a boy with his pants down.

*

On a date, always take a dime, a pin and a telephone book. (The book runs interference in case you have to sit on his lap.)

*

Watch out when he takes off his glasses.

*

Most men never get much older than twelve.

*

All I can tell you about sex is that you both take off all of your clothes.

Bloomers kept Grandma from going to seed.

*

Never fake anything except adoration.

*

A Nashville man is a Bible-thumpin', guitar-plunkin', beer-dunkin', woman-humpin' man.

The elderly couple, who had been living together for forty years, was still scandal material for the small Indiana community where my parents lived. When Grandma came to visit, Mom calmly explained the situation to her, because they would all be at the same party later that evening.

With great anticipation, Grandma finally met the woman and her short, wrinkled, balding companion. Grandma took one look and whispered to Mother, "Now I understand why she didn't want to marry him."

—E.B.

Health

2

A Spritz, A Blitz
And A Sitz

Orientation week at the small Southern college was filled with endless registration lines, conferences and generalized bedlam. So when my roommate found a note to report to the Student Health Center, she didn't give it much thought.

Her first free moment came three days later, after she attended Yom Kippur services at a nearby synagogue. Like most Jews, she had been fasting since sundown the previous day.

Explaining that the health report necessary for admission lacked a urinalysis, the nurse promptly ushered Sally into the bathroom. And there she sat, embarrassed, knowing her efforts would be futile because she had drunk no water for eighteen hours. After twenty-five minutes she emerged, empty-handed. By now several nurses and doctors had gathered for a coffee break.

Ordinarily my shy roommate would have run for the nearest exit. But remembering her mother's words of wisdom — "Be proud of your religion and take time to explain it." — she nervously approached the waiting crowd. "I'm sorry, but I couldn't go to the bathroom. It's Yom Kippur."

"It's what?"

"Yom Kippur. Today is a Jewish holiday, and I won't be able to go to the bathroom."

Everyone stared at her. The head nurse loudly replied, "That's horrible! You mean it's against your religion to go to the bathroom today?"

For the next four years, neither flu, hives, mononucleosis nor unfulfilled urinalysis could lure Sally back to the Student Health Center, and she was half-convinced that the Chancellor would publicly withhold her diploma at the graduation exercises while everyone waited for her to complete the requirement.

—L.A.

✻

Always wear clean underwear in case you're in an accident.

✻

If you suck your thumb, you'll have to marry an orthodontist.

✻

If you want to get out of an A-cup, hold a rubber ball in each hand and squeeze it fifty times in the morning and fifty times at night. If nothing else, it will improve your tennis grip.

✻

When you drive past a hospital, hold your breath so you won't catch anything.

✻

Your bosoms aren't too big. As long as you can't throw one over each shoulder, I wouldn't worry about it.

My friend's mother went to her gynecologist for her yearly check-up. Right before her examination, she was required to go to the bathroom. Unfortunately, there was no toilet paper, so she reached into her purse and substituted a Kleenex.

When she emerged from the bathroom, the nurse showed her into the examining room, told her to take off her clothes, lie down on the table and put her feet up into the stirrups. In a few moments the doctor came in and greeted her. He sat down ready to begin his examination. Suddenly he burst out laughing. Medical school and even twenty-five years of experience as a physician had not prepared this man for the sight that greeted him. He had examined hundreds of women, but had never before viewed a woman decorated with a row of S&H Green Stamps.

—L.A.

Childbirth is the only time you can scream your head off and no one will think you are fooling.

*

Any man who says labor pains are all in your head has a rotten sense of direction.

*

Kiss through Kleenex.

*

Take a dose of sulphur and molasses every spring to clean out the winter.

*

We didn't intend for you to have quite so much of Daddy's nose. But don't worry, the doctor can fix it.

When I was a girl, pot was something you sat on.

*

Don't worry, the doctor isn't looking at you when he's examining you. Where another man might see your nose, the doctor sees your nostrils.

*

If you don't wear a bra when you play tennis, you could get a bad case of whiplash.

*

Don't complain. It's not a bad headache until you have to look in your hand to see if your eyeballs have fallen out.

*

Psychiatrists deal with mental gore.

*

Don't ask anyone how they feel — they'll tell you.

*

When I had my hysterectomy, they removed the baby buggy but left in the playpen.

*

If worrying burned up calories, I'd be a size 5.

*

Smoking a cigarette may not hurt you, but grounding you will.

*

Your mother should always have a key to your apartment, in case you get sick.

*

If you don't wear a bra now, you'll need a crane later.

If you want to be physically fit, put on your sneakers and wash the floor for me.

17

One day the phone rang. I answered, and the woman on the other end asked, "Is the doctor there?" Since my husband is a Ph.D. and not an M.D., I suspected she had the wrong number. I replied, "Which doctor do you want to speak with?"

"Dr. Blumenfeld, the urologist," she replied. I told her that she had the wrong number. She insisted. "This can't be the wrong number, it's the one my doctor told me to call. Are you sure there is no Dr. Blumenfeld at this number?" I told her there *was* a Dr. Blumenfeld at the number she had called, but that he was a psychologist. "What's that?" she asked.

"Lady," I said, "I can assure you it's not at all like a urologist. As a matter of fact, my husband can't even fix a dripping faucet." She never called back.

—E.B.

Your nose has been in this family for generations; I don't know why you want to change it.

*

Take out your retainer before you kiss a boy.

*

Grandma's cure-all: spritz one end, blitz the other and then sitz awhile.

*

Chicken soup is good for anything but the chicken.

*

Your child isn't sick; all you need to do is clean out his liver.

*

A model may look great in clothes, but underneath she's just as flat as a fritter.

Natural childbirth is unnatural.

*

The doctor inflated a balloon up my behind, shook my hand and charged me two hundred dollars. Isn't modern medicine wonderful?

*

I'm glad you stopped biting your fingernails. Now go cut them.

*

A husband with a cold is like a baby with colic. They get cranky and you get tired.

*

So you're taking birth control pills. Well, if you want to be a sex maniac, I guess that's what you'll have to do.

In spite of having a son and a son-in-law who are physicians, Mother thinks doctors are wonderful for everyone but herself. Wearying of a constant barrage of nagging by well-meaning friends, who were concerned merely because fifteen years had elapsed since her last physical, she relented and made an appointment.

Time brings about changes and improvements in technique, and Mother was definitely out of step after so many years. She was ushered into a sterile inner sanctum, while the nurse stood in the doorway with a pencil poised over a writing pad and said, in her clinical manner, "Are you having a Pap Smear?"

Horrified, Mother gasped, "What? A Pabst Beer at nine o'clock in the morning? I should say not! But I *will* have a Coke, if you don't mind."

—L.A.

If you have trouble getting pregnant, stand on your head after having sex.

☀

Sleeping is my favorite exercise.

My cousin knew that her mother would be uncomfortable discussing birth control methods with her, so she went to a friend's mother who was a gynecologist. "Doctor," she asked, "could you please explain ovation to me?"

The doctor looked up from her desk and, with a deadpan expression she could only have learned in medical school, said, "I believe you mean ovulation. The ovation comes later."

—E.B.

Marriage

3

*There's A Dead Horse
In My Bedroom*

Aunt Lucille and Uncle Bill had been married for fifty years — always a very warm and loving relationship. One day I happened upon them while they were sitting on a sofa. They were sitting close together, engrossed in conversation and touching one another.

I was moved by this scene and told them how beautiful I thought it was that, after all these years, they were still holding hands. Whereupon Aunt Lucille remarked, in her old New Orleans fashion, "Honey, if we ever let go, we'll kill each other."

—E.B.

You've never picked out a dress by yourself. How can you pick out a husband?

*

The second wife always has a cleaning lady.

*

"There's a goon for every goon," was said when I wondered if Mr. Right would *ever* come along. Happily, my goon eventually did.

*

On your wedding night, don't worry if his face turns red. He isn't having a heart attack.

*

The secret to a happy marriage is never sit down together for a serious talk.

*

If you want to be a good wife, always do everything your husband says. But you don't always have to be a good wife.

*

When you have an argument with your husband, don't drag things out of your mental museum.

*

Now I know your marriage will last. You've been together long enough to be on your second bottle of Tabasco sauce.

*

Marriage is a lot of hard work and a lot of luck, because you never know if you've married a mashuganah.
(A mashuganah is a rare tropical bird sometimes found nesting in kosher delicatessens.)

Although my husband speaks no Spanish, he was invited to lecture at the University of Mexico on research methodology. His expertise was valued even though it required an interpreter. Warren studied the Spanish-English dictionary until he felt he had selected just the right title for his scientific speech. He wrote it in Spanish on a large poster to be displayed outside the lecture hall. I knew he had a good title, because the poster attracted so many people that the crowd filled the room and flowed into the hall.

After the speech was over, the beautiful Mexican interpreter said to me, "My mother is never going to believe it when I tell her the title of Professor Blumenfeld's lecture." Becoming suspicious, I asked her to read what the poster said. She translated: "It says, 'Attention Students: There's a dead horse in my bedroom.'"

—E.B.

It's easier to find a good horse than a good husband, because you know the horse will never turn into a jackass.

✳

A wife has to have selective hearing.

✳

Marry for love, but be sure he has plenty of money.

✳

All I ever got out of this marriage is dishes, grease and garbage — and, of course, my children.

✳

When I got a divorce, I had a face lift. It was cheaper than a nervous breakdown.

23

T he weekend, I thought, could not get worse. We had flown North in a January blizzard for a funeral and were staying in a motel. My husband and I were grief-stricken. The weather was unbearable, our little girl was upset and our son had the flu. Exhaustion had finally put the others to sleep, but all the snoring, worrying and wheezing kept me wide awake.

Suddenly I heard a bell clanging and a persistent knock at the door. My family slept on as I opened the door to find a smoky hallway and a fireman announcing, "Something on this floor is burning. You don't need to evacuate yet, but stay awake until we locate the cause. We'll let you know if you have to escape."

I frantically tried to wake my husband. My mind was racing as I considered what clothes to throw on everyone, what important items to grab, how to bundle up our sick child and how to unlock the patio door. When my helpful husband finally woke up, I told him in a calm but urgent voice what the fireman had said. He listened politely, replied, "OK," and turned over and went back to sleep.

—L.A.

Don't discuss anything with your husband until he has downed his first cup of coffee.

*

A trial separation is a separation for him and a trial for you.

*

Truth is the cornerstone of divorce.

*

Sometimes I think I should go out and have a meaningless affair.

A smart man will marry a dumb blonde, if she's smart.

*

Canasta is more fun than sex. Anything is more fun than sex.

Some mothers are avid collectors of memorabilia. My friend's mother was so sentimental about her daughter's accomplishments that I was convinced she still had the Kleenex commemorating her baby's first stuffy nose.

When my friend got married, she sent her mother a postcard from her honeymoon which simply read: "It's wonderful."

The years passed. On my friend's tenth wedding anniversary, she opened her mailbox and found the same postcard she had written years ago. However, two little words had been added. Her mother ask___ _____ _at's wonderful?"

—E.B.

He divorced me because he wanted _____ self. Now he doesn't like what he found.

It doesn't matter whe____ ____ or jockey shorts. What matters is what ____

If a husband and wife are ____ two theater tickets?

Not telling your husband is not ____

Save yourself until you're married. The____ go to it.

25

> My friend's mother felt that she should give her daughter some belated advice the night before her wedding. She tried hard to think of just the right words, but nothing came. All she could think to tell her child was, "Remember, Rome wasn't built in a day."
>
> The wedding took place, and the young couple left for their honeymoon. A week later the bride's mother received a postcard. On it were written four little words: "Rome was finally built."
>
> —E.B.

Now that you've been on your honeymoon, I can tell you this joke.

*

If he's in the mood, the dishes can wait.

*

My wedding was not mine, it was my mother's. Yours will be mine.

*

Married children fight — they come tell Mother. Mother goes crazy — children go to bed.

*

If a couple can manage to have an amiable divorce, they don't need one.

*

If you are going to marry a soldier of lower rank than yours, never wear your stripes to bed.

*

Look for a man with no parents.

Don't tell me any arguments between you and your husband, because you'll kiss and make up, and I'll still hate him.

Don't worry if your honeymoon isn't exactly what the book says. It isn't the final exam.

✳

Revenge puts bloom in the cheeks.

✳

It doesn't pay to spend fifty dollars on a nightgown, because the first thing your husband will say is, "Take it off."

✳

Don't bother him with nitty-gritty things. Or important things that are none of his business.

For me, the second most unpleasant experience in the world is quarreling with my husband. The first is meeting a woman who claims that she and her mate never disagree about anything. Although arguments with my husband are rare, they do occur. But only one gave me any degree of satisfaction.

I don't remember what, as a newlywed, our very first argument was about, but I do remember being very frustrated at the outcome. My husband was calmer, more logical, and worst of all... completely right. I knew that I couldn't go through life with a man who thought he had gotten the best of me. Painstakingly I made arrangements and planned revenge.

Exactly two weeks after our celebrated first fight, Warren received a congratulatory letter. It stated that his application had been accepted, his opponent had been chosen, and the date had been set. He was a middle-weight contender for the Chicago Golden Gloves.

—E.B.

I'm glad to see that my son is getting smart enough to pick a woman like you and stop going after just another pretty face.

*

When your husband snores, don't poke him. Give him a loving pat. It could lead to something better.

*

Act like a lady until you get married. Then you can let him have it.

*

Never tell him how much things cost. That way he'll live longer.

*

After you get married, make your husband a pleasant person.

Children 4

I Pray For Boredom But It Never Comes

My mother-in-law is a dear lady whose comments I value. So when she advised me about my son Josh, I listened. "A mother must let her child experience new things," she said.

I thought of this when he turned our bathroom into a chemistry lab; when his hermit crab pinched my finger; when his gerbil chewed through the sofa. I thought of it when his goldfish flew out of the bowl for lack of oxygen and when his model plane collection filled our kitchen.

But when the exterminator warned us that the bug collection could spread, I approached this gentle lady for consolation and asked if she had let *her* son do all of these things. She replied with a loving look, "Heck no! What do you think I am...crazy?"

Here's to all those dear ladies who give crazy advice about children and to the crazier ones who listen.

—E.B.

Don't brag about your children to your friends. If yours are smarter, they'll be embarrassed. If theirs are smarter, they won't be impressed.

*

I used to have three theories for raising children. But when I had three children, I lost all the theories.

*

It's all right for me to spoil them. I'm their grandmother, and I'm supposed to.

*

You've outgrown my lap, but you'll never outgrow my heart.

*

Mothers aren't supposed to see everything.

*

I've raised girls and I've raised boys. Girls eventually outgrow temper tantrums, but boys, they just get worse and worse until finally you call it "mannish."

*

Rhythm doesn't work. (Mother of ten)

*

Have only one child, and you won't have anyone fighting over the bone.

*

Only have two children, because one will go to the East coast, one will go to the West coast. And if you have a third, she'll go to Canada, and you'll never have any peace.

*

There's nothing sweeter than the patter of little feet...going home.

My friend is a naturally outgoing person who enjoys sharing her experiences. Thus, when she was in college, she felt that to give her parents their money's worth, it was her duty as well as her pleasure to share with them the details of her activities at the end of each day. She left no word unturned as she regaled them with tales of classes, tests, friends and parties, knowing well the joy it brought her parents.

One evening, arriving home later than usual, she spent two hours sitting on the edge of their bed talking animatedly. After returning to her room, she remembered something she forgot to tell them. But she found the door locked.

The next morning she and her mother were reminiscing about the early days of her parents' courtship, and my friend teased, "Well, Mama, you're always telling me what a great lover Daddy was when he was younger."

"He still would be," Mama replied tartly, "if his eldest daughter didn't bang on our door in the middle of the night."

—L.A.

My children: I wouldn't buy them for a penny, but I wouldn't sell them for a million.

*

I know more than you about raising children. After all, I'm a grandmother, and nothing is higher than a grandmother.

*

You were always a source of repressed pride.

*

My children must love me — they call me collect.

Take that book on child psychology and apply it to the seat of his pants.

*

When educating our children, it is my husband's job to talk about sex and driving. Whichever comes first.

*

When I said you were my only hope for grandchildren, I didn't mean you should keep churning them out.

*

When your children are small, you have small problems. When they are big, big problems. But the biggest and hardest problem of all is when they get married, and you have to keep your mouth shut.

*

Even the mothers of apes think their children are beautiful.

While I was helping out in my son's class at school, his teacher shared with me some papers the children had written concerning their goals in life. My favorite was from an ambitious thirteen-year-old, who wrote: "Twenty years from now I will be thirty-three. I will be living in Virginia, right outside Washington D.C., near Mount Vernon. My house will be an old Williamsburg colonial-style house. It will be Williamsburg blue and a creamy yellow. In my house I will live with my husband, my daughter, my son and our two dogs.

"I will be a Senator. When Congress is not in session, I will work in an office on the upper floor of a bank. I will have a lot of power and lots of people will ask for my advice. When I'm not working, I'll just relax with my family. Sometimes I wonder if I wouldn't have been happier as a tour guide."

—E.B.

When you have a baby, you'll have two children: the baby and your husband.

35

Grandchildren were made for young people.

*

Your father could train our dog better than you raise your children.

*

I am going to teach your children to do to you exactly what you're doing to me.

*

Little babies are big tyrants.

*

An adopted baby is a wanted baby, which gives it an unfair advantage over a lot of other children.

*

What's so wrong about naming your baby "Pinkney"? It was good enough for Grandpa.

*

Sometimes you feel like hugging them, and sometimes you feel like killing them. But who has time for funerals?

*

What is this nonsense about waiting until a child can tell you he is ready to go potty?

*

When you get married, girl, are you going to get it! You are going to have four of yourself.

*

There's no such thing as a perfect child. Remember you are not molding clay here.

All children are born with a hearing problem. They can hear everyone's mother but their own.

*

Mother-daughter dresses are cute. For about five minutes.

*

You're not old enough to be wise.

T o the grade school child, permission slips are second in importance only to recess. Most parents sign these escapes from tedium automatically. My neighbor Edith was no exception.

She was taken aback, however, when she realized the nature of the most recent note. Her daughter's health class was going to be shown a movie on VD.

She interrupted her freckle-faced, gum-chewing child watching television. As nonchalantly as possible, she asked, "Dear, do you know what VD is?" The girl answered, "Oh, everyone knows what that is." "Well," Mother persisted, "I think I'd like you to tell me."

The child stood on her head, and with an exasperated sigh, said, "Oh, *Mother*, it's Virgin's Disease." Edith signed the slip.

—E.B.

Your children are not letting me talk to *my* children!

*

Fresh flowers are acceptable. Fresh mouths are not.

*

If your child doesn't fall out of bed by the time he is three, you are an overprotective mother.

Religion, Politics And Philosophy

5

Pray To God But Vote
A Straight Party Ticket

The American political system is especially precious to new citizens who have come from lands of persecution. My grandmother, no exception, always encouraged me to be politically active. She especially loved the excitement preceding a presidential election.

So when the Democratic Party had its national convention in Chicago, I took her to the platform proceedings. She was thrilled to mingle in the crowded hotel lobby and excitedly identified her congressional heroes.

On the way home, I said, "Grandma, what did you like the best?" And she answered, "I liked the best when Senator Sparkman spoke to me. Only in

America would a United States Senator speak to a regular person."

Amazed, I asked, "Grandma, when did Senator Sparkman speak to you?"

She answered, "When I stepped on his foot."

—E.B.

✣

Never argue about politics or religion unless you think you are right.

✣

When it comes to politics, don't argue, listen to your husband. But when you get into that little booth, pull the curtain shut and vote for anyone you damn well please.

✣

If a woman doctor can heal my body, I guess a woman minister can try my soul.

✣

How come people go to shows on time, go to dances on time, but always come late to church?

✣

Quit worrying about erroneous zones, pulling your own strings, being your own best friend and that meditation stuff. Just do what I say and it will all work out.

✣

There may be some truly holy men in the world today, but Mahatma Gandhi would never have hawked flowers on street corners.

✣

So the weather is bad — it's not for you alone.

It was a typical pre-air conditioning Missouri day. All the neighbors were sitting on their porch swings watching the steam rise from the pores of the sidewalk which stretched in front of our neat little white houses. I was in the kitchen helping Mother squeeze lemons when there was a knock at our front door. Standing there was a seedy-looking man wearing baggy pants and a straw hat. He informed Mother that the carnival had broken up and the Geek had no place to go. And, since the Geek was Jewish, he was going to leave him with my father, the town's rabbi.

I was delighted. The Geek was a sideshow attraction most children weren't allowed to see, since his act consisted of biting off the heads of live chickens.

All Mother could say was, "He doesn't *look* Jewish." But before she could protest any further, the seedy man departed, leaving a pathetic shopworn carnival attraction sitting on our front steps.

Mother's version of the end of the story was that Dad located some of the carny's relatives in Philadelphia, and my folks provided him with a bus ticket to get there. But in my heart I always knew that the Geek stayed in that small Missouri town, developed a taste for chicken salad and became president of my father's congregation.

—E.B.

People who gamble on a good deal end up with a good deal less.

*

Sex with your husband is your Christian duty.

*

You won't find a perfect religion because of the imperfect people who practice it.

Our minister found a new source of energy. His sermon propelled me right out of church.

*

Don't vote for her just because she's a woman, but don't let that stop you either.

*

I am the world's foremost authority on my own opinion.

*

If all the feminists pursue careers instead of families, the next generation won't have any feminists, and we'll have to start all over again.

*

Don't believe the statistics unless you know the statistician.

*

Slogans let the ignorant think they understand what's going on.

*

Looking at the world situation, the average person has a choice between apathy and ulcers.

*

He's still your father even if he voted for Roosevelt.

*

The next time you take Communion, take your gum out first.

*

In a political discussion, it is a mistake to assume that the other person is rational.

*

When you go to Confession, don't forget to check your little laundry list of sins.

Life's dessert is a wait-and-see pudding.

*

I don't understand how Moses was ready to leave Egypt in only one day, when it takes me four weeks just to make the Passover meal.

*

Easter is a time for Jesus, rebirth and those God-awful eggs.

My friend didn't quite know how to tell her parents about her engagement, because her fiancé was a Hindu student from Nepal, where everyone in his caste was born in a position of religious leadership. Her very Catholic mother dropped the phone when my friend finally called and announced, "Mom, guess what! I'm going to marry a priest."

—E.B.

Jesus was born before his time.

*

My opinion is uncluttered by facts.

*

If you have to ask the rabbi, it isn't kosher.

*

After he drops all those words, be careful where you step.

*

Voting used to be the one thing men could do for themselves. Now men expect women to do that for them, too.

*

The truth is the truth, but I don't want to believe it.

The male ego cannot be legislated away.

*

The more you stir a stink, the more it stinks.

*

There is no substitute for incomprehensible good luck.

*

The worst kind of pollution is verbiage garbage.

*

More people have died from bigotry than any other disease.

*

If the American Indian hadn't trusted foreigners, none of us would be here.

*

Go to church. Look what science did to your father.

*

It's a wonder more people don't pray when they need help. It's quick, it's easy and it's free.

*

In this world it rains on the Just and the Unjust alike, but the Unjusts have the Justs' umbrellas.

*

When are you going to grow out of being politically active?

*

We didn't all come over on the same ship, but we're all in the same boat.

*

A political party can't fly with a candidate who's a lead balloon.

Transcendental meditation is for the birds.

The woman had just received an award as Mother of the Year at a Catholic school in a small Indiana community. She was very excited about the honor and about introducing my father, a rabbi, as the keynote speaker of the evening.

After an effusive introduction, she concluded with, "And now, I am pleased to present Father Richter." As he rose, my mother blurted out, "Biologically, yes — theologically, no."

—E.B.

Priests and rabbis never have first names.

*

Freedom of speech is for everyone, but you have the right not to listen.

*

Civilization is the only thing that can move backwards and forwards at the same time.

*

If you go through life contemplating your navel, you'll end up with a narrow mind and a stiff neck.

*

Sometimes I think civilization is a passing fancy.

Growing Older

6

I'm Going To Live Until Halley's Comet Comes Again

For my neighbor Phyllis's fiftieth birthday, her seventy-two-year-old mother treated her to lunch at a fancy department store. In spite of their oil and vinegar relationship, the celebration was going well. That is, until they finished dessert.

"Thank you, Mother, the lunch was delicious. Now let's go to the shoe department and look around."

"Oh, no, Phyllis, we can't go."

"Why not?"

"Because," her mother insisted, "you haven't gone to the bathroom yet."

"I don't *have* to go to the bathroom!"

"Now, Phyllis, you know how you are."

Their loud voices attracted attention, and propriety finally won out over anger. But Phyllis wasted no time in retaliation. At the cashier's table, where

47

oversized lollipops were for sale, she grabbed the biggest one, tugged on her mother's sleeve, and in her best Shirley Temple voice, begged, "Oh, please, Mommy, could I have a lollipop? Could I please?"

Her mother waved her off. "Phyllis, you're causing a scene!" When Phyllis defiantly unwrapped the candy and licked it, her mother shook her head in resignation, turned to the cashier and said disgustedly, "Oh, let her have it. It's her birthday."

—E.B.

*

My mother and I would not have had any trouble between us if she had understood that I was fully grown at six.

*

It's better to wear out than rust out.

*

Why should I go to Europe? That's where I came from.

*

When you're young, it's called sassy. When you're old, it's called gumption.

*

Learn to play bridge so your mind won't shrivel up when you're old.

*

My memory is shorter than a chigger's navel.

*

As we grow older, God dims our vision so we can't see the dust.

*

I want my tombstone to read, "My mom will do it."

The only reasonable way to cope with turning thirty is to hide all day in the closet.

*

Sixty is old enough for anyone to ever be. Then you count backwards.

*

The advantage of never having been beautiful is that no one can ever say, "Guess who I saw on the street today? Ruth Miller. She used to be so gorgeous, and you ought to see her now!"

*

People don't get better or worse, they only get more-so.

*

Gray hair inspires respect, but it sure doesn't inspire passion.

I was twenty-two when I got married, a respectable not-too-old-not-too-young age for a bride back then. My husband, four years older, sometimes referred to me in jest as his child bride. In the next few years, whenever anyone asked Bob how old I was, he would gush, "Oh, to me she'll always be twenty-two." I appreciated the sentiment, if not the reality.

Then one evening shortly after my thirty-fifth birthday, we had dinner with some new friends. Discussing colleges and possible friends in common, the man asked Bob how old I was. Romantically he sighed, "Oh, to me she'll always be thirty."

I can just hear him now, walking along some beach resort in our retirement years telling someone, "Oh, to me she'll always be sixty-three!"

—L.A.

Since I've had my face lift, people tell me I don't look a day over sixty.

✳

Gray hair looks distinguished. I just don't want to look extinguished.

✳

When a grandma turned eighty-five, her granddaughter asked, "How old were you when you stopped having sex?" "My God," she replied, "Ask someone older than me."

✳

I don't mind getting older. I just mind that I have aging children.

✳

The worst thing about growing old is looking as old as the people you graduated from high school with.

✳

Somewhere between your first childhood and my second, I hope there will be a period of grace where we can just be friends.

✳

When your father died, I became a regenerated virgin.

✳

I'm as old as my tongue and a little older than my teeth.

✳

I have a twenty-five-year-old mind trapped in a sixty-five-year-old body.

✳

Don't believe all those books about old people having sex. It isn't true.

✳

I want to see an X-rated movie before I die, but I'm not old enough yet.

The older you get, the harder it is to lose weight, because your body has made friends with your fat.

Mother was invited to a large bridge party where she knew only the hosts. To remember the names of the other guests, she tried associating husbands and wives in her mind. When they sat down to play, however, Mom discovered that her opponent was a woman whose husband she didn't recall meeting. So she inquired in her politest voice, "I beg your pardon, but are you a loose woman?"
—L.A.

Die in your own bed — not someone else's.

*

If you can't remember how old you are, ask your husband. He will remember immediately.

*

Seeing an attractive man only reminds me of how droopy my eyelids are.

*

You live and learn and then you die and forget it all.

*

She has a disco back and a mausoleum front.

*

Anybody who says life begins at sixty must have been asleep for the first fifty-nine years.

*

After forty, life is just a physical maintenance job.

*

I thought I was old the first time someone called me "ma'am." But I *knew* I was old the first time a young doctor called me by my first name, and I resented his brashness.

Friends And Relatives

7

A Picnic With Your Relatives Is No Picnic

Grandmother has always encouraged Mother to be assertive, and sometimes the rewards are unexpected. One night at a restaurant in Houston, Mother spied a lady she thought was an old friend of Grandmother's from Dallas. Taking her courage in hand, she went over to speak to the woman and said, "Aren't you Gertie Couples from Dallas?"

The woman wasn't, but she was gracious enough to put Mother at ease. "Is your mother from Dallas?" she asked politely.

"No, she's originally from St. Louis."

"Did you say St. Louis?"

"Yes."

"What was your mother's family name? I once lived in St. Louis."

"Lieber," Mother said.

"Arthur Lieber?" the woman asked, her face lighting up.
"My uncle," Mother replied.
"I used to go with your uncle. Sit down, girl, and have a drink!"
                                                                    —L.A.

*

With relatives, long distance is even better than being there.

*

Even if he's wrong a lot, he's still your father.

*

Be careful. Strange animals might bite, kick or carry disease. Come to think of it, so might some of your friends.

*

Never create a situation which will leave someone feeling like a fool, such as asking, "What's new?"

My mother has the kind of looks that grow on you. In other words, she never made the finals for Miss Cotton-Pickin' Texas of 1937. It didn't concern her much, but one day over lunch her good friend Ceil was considering it. "You know, Ruth," she remarked, "it's really funny how people can get better looking the more you like them. Take you, for instance. I really think you're beautiful, and God knows you're not!"
    With friends like that, who needs relatives?
                                                                    —L.A.

He must have gotten kicked in the head by a pigeon at an early age.

Our wedding reception was proceeding well until it was time to throw the bouquet. The photographer was busy posing everyone, when my mother's best friend took me aside. "Don't throw the flowers up over your head, like I did. They don't have much weight and will go straight up and land on your head. Throw them sideways around your body." Raised to respect my elders, and bowing to this woman's multiple experiences in the field, I obeyed.

She neglected, however, to consider my tennis arm. When the photographer gave the signal, thinking the bouquet would float like a posy of feathers, I hurled it like a discus.

The first throw hit the ceiling, thirty feet above. The second toss came to rest near the buffet table, nowhere near the by-now restless maidens. My final throw whizzed over the heads of the leaping girls, missed the punch bowl by inches and landed in the arms of a very surprised bartender. He took one look at the flowery omen and exclaimed, "But I'm already married!"

—L.A.

If you are ever in a jam and don't want to answer, look thoughtfully into their eyes and say, "Why do you ask?"

✳

The only people who don't have any problems are the ones who haven't told you yet.

✳

Your father is a mean guy with a nice streak.

✳

I don't know. Ask your father. He doesn't know either, but he'll give you an answer.

Inside your grandmother is a warm person struggling to get out.

*

You're the kind of child I always told you not to play with.

*

Everybody's business is nobody's business.

*

If you're raised on skunks, you hanker fer 'em.

*

Whenever Grandmother observed someone she perceived as lacking taste in clothing or jewelry, in spite of huge sums of money spent, she would roll her eyes toward heaven and say, "God gives candy to people who have no teeth."

*

I'm not a back seat driver, but sometimes your father likes me to tell him how to drive.

*

Treat your family like friends and your friends like family.

*

You invited twelve lawyers to the party. No wonder it was dull.

*

Never invite more than one doctor to a dinner party, unless you want viscerals discussed openly.

*

Familiarity breeds disgust.

*

Don't look at Cousin Irving when he puts on his underwear.

Narrow-minded people are like narrow-necked bottles...the less they have in them, the more noise they make pouring it out.

The reason you have so many brothers and sisters is because when something breaks, we always need a youngest to blame.

✻

Mothers-in-law aren't half bad if you go three-quarters of the way.

✻

Sometimes the best thing you can do is just listen. Other times the best thing you can do is not to.

✻

Your father is so handy around the house, he is able to fix the same thing over and over again.

✻

When Grandma comes to visit, hide your boyfriend.

✻

Like mother, like son: he's a real fruit of the womb.

✻

If you want to keep a friend, never suggest what's wrong with her children.

✻

Don't ever have a guest room.

✻

She can't help being ugly, but she could stay at home.

✻

In our family, knock on wood, there are no drunkards, no lawyers and no Capricorns.

✻

Sometimes I think the only thing you and I have in common is your father.

Some relatives gossip, some always show up at mealtime and others are unmentionable. But in my family one of the most frequently mentioned relatives is my great-aunt Bea. She has a big heart, but when she visits anyone's home she feels compelled to nose around the bathroom and mentally grade them on cleanliness, decor and neatness.

One Thanksgiving Aunt Bea made her usual pilgrimage to our bathroom. It was tidy enough, but the shower curtain was closed across the four-foot expanse of tub. Expecting to see the proof of our slobhood lurking in the tub, she flung the curtain aside.

Instead, hanging on the wall was a huge poster, painstakingly lettered, painted and glittered. It said: "Hello, Aunt Bea! Do we pass inspection?"

She didn't come out for quite some time.

—L.A.

Act normal in front of the relatives.

*

Sometimes I forget and think he's my son — and you're my daughter-in-law.

*

If you can't get it from Grandmother, you can't get it.

*

If you want to keep a secret, find out first where I'm having lunch and go somewhere else.

*

If you don't mind, I won't tell our Philadelphia relatives about your divorce.

*

Never mention a rope to a family that has had a hanging.

At the St. Louis World's Fair in 1907, my great-aunt Emily was walking through a long exhibition hall. She saw someone approaching who looked very familiar. Aunt Emily waved; the woman waved. Aunt Emily smiled; the woman smiled. Then Aunt Emily ran smack into the mirror.

—L.A.

Food

8

Never Serve Aspic To A Meat And Potatoes Man

As a new bride, I was not always lucky with the food I prepared. The most difficult task was coordinating a meal so that the vegetables and potatoes wouldn't still be cooking after we had finished dessert.

My husband was a graduate student. He usually had his mind on his studies and his nose buried in a book, so he didn't notice all of my mistakes. But even though I followed Mother's instructions faithfully, I couldn't hide the disaster of my first meatloaf.

I almost got away with it, but as he began to drink his second cupful, he wanted to know what it was. And when he asked how it got that way, I didn't have an answer. I still don't know because I've never been able to duplicate the recipe. I can, however, fix a terrific fried roast beef.

—E.B.

To make good chicken soup, the first thing you do is you don't go to the A&P and buy a dead chicken.

✻

If you eat chocolate mousse, your legs will grow together.

✻

I eat junk food to get it out of the house.

✻

The cleaner the delicatessen, the worse the food.

✻

Eat — you'll feed your training bra.

✻

Stick-to-your-ribs food is really stick-to-your-hips food.

✻

Garlic is good for you, so eat it and don't worry that your husband may not make love to you. He can always turn his back.

✻

If you really want to know if I boiled the eggs long enough, walk up five flights and throw them off the roof. Then you'll know.

✻

His greatest joy is eating a good meal. My greatest joy is not having to cook it.

✻

Eat. You can diet in *your* home.

✻

Don't worry if your cake falls apart. Layer it with ice cream in a parfait glass, call it Devil's Surprise, and everyone will want the recipe.

When cooking crab, be sure to remove a certain part or you'll die.

*

If you eat one pea, you can have another.

*

Don't ask a good cook for her recipe. Just measure the size of her hands.

*

Don't bother to eat. Just apply it directly to your thighs.

*

A piece apiece and two for Pa.

*

When I diet, I nibble myself to death.

*

Mixing soup cans with chicken is not gourmet cooking. It's not even good cooking. But once a week you can get away with it.

My cousin had never been interested in her mother's cooking tips. Now she was preparing for her first dinner party with great difficulty. Two hours before arrival time her mother dropped by, finding her daughter sobbing over a bowl of strawberries. "Oh, Mother, how can anyone like to cook? I've spent all afternoon cleaning these strawberries with my tweezer, and I *still* can't get all the little stickers out."

—L.A.

If he tells you one more time that your cooking isn't as good as his mother's, remind him that his father has ulcers.

Forget trying to cook like his mother. You can follow her recipes, but you can't stir in the memories.

*

If his mother was such a good cook, why was he so thin before he married you?

*

Don't talk about pork at Cousin Jenny's house.

*

Why are you eating the bread? You know what bread tastes like.

*

Eating pasta will thicken you up.

*

Cook your vegetables till they're tender as a baby's behind.

*

You can spend four hours baking a beautiful cake and the company will rave. You can spend five minutes buying a beautiful cake and the company will rave.

My mother found an aging sardine in the back of the refrigerator. Always preaching that it is sinful to waste food, she hid it amidst a large assortment of cheeses, vegetables, meats and other garnishes on a tray for her party that evening.

The first person at the buffet table was Grandma. She spied the sardine, popped it into her mouth, spit it out and shouted, "Nobody touch anything! The dinner's poisoned!"

—E.B.

There are only a dozen left. They shouldn't go to waste. Eat.

Cooking is easy. You use a fistful of this and a fistful of that, and then you improvise.

*

You're not too fat. You're just too short.

*

To make sure a haddock is fresh, buy it with its head on and look it right in the eye.

*

What you eat today walks and talks tomorrow.

*

Take pride in your appearance. Would you like another brownie?

*

You should always cook enough for fourteen people — in case they drop by.

*

If you exercise and lose some weight, then the boys will invite you out to eat.

*

Don't eat standing up or your legs will get fat.

*

If you haven't started dinner, fry an onion because it smells so promising.

*

If you can read, you can cook.

A young bride I know called her mother long distance. She was thoroughly disgusted. "Mother," she said, "I don't know why they call a soft-boiled egg a three-minute egg when it takes twenty minutes to cook." Her mother asked her to describe her procedure. It went like this: "Well, I plug in the electric frying pan, put in some water and push the poor little thing around until it's ready. Isn't that the way you do it?"

—E.B.

Grooming And Manners

9

Nice Girls Wear Girdles

In the small town where I grew up, we could dress as elegantly as we wanted, but there weren't many places to go. One summer Mother's sophisticated cousin from New York came to visit. We were in a tizzy trying to plan activities for her, and Mother decided we should take her out to dinner at least once during her stay.

The restaurants were few, so we took Herta to the only one in town that had pretensions of being French. Mother was very anxious that Herta approve and watched her nervously.

Herta, enfurred in mink and a designer original, took in the room wordlessly. With great effort she ignored the maitre d' nibbling on her gloved hand. She raised a meticulously groomed eyebrow at the red flocked wallpaper, which almost covered the previous owner's bullfighting mural, and still said nothing. She even overlooked the waiter's arrogant flings at French which filtered through his Midwestern twang. The slipshod service, however, was more than poor Herta could bear.

After three requests failed to prod the waiter to bring our drinks, Cousin Herta beckoned to the maitre d' with a bejeweled hand and a steely smile. Obviously expecting a compliment, he hurried over to our table and bowed regally. "I just want to ask you one question," Herta said ever-so-sweetly. "If I die of thirst, will it destroy the ambience?"

—E.B.

*

After sex, the second best feeling in the world is taking off your girdle.

*

So Grandma crocheted you a bikini. It's a shame you couldn't wait until she finished it.

*

Don't let a man ring up your Kotex in the drugstore.

*

Nice girls undress in the closet, never in front of a mirror.

*

Take your money out of your purse and put it in your bra. On second thought, you'd be sure to lose it in there.

*

Wear underpants to bed in case there's a fire.

*

Clean your room or the Board of Health will condemn it.

Dress each day as if you are going to meet Mr. Right. If you don't meet him, you might meet his family.

> **M**y mother, a very formal and proper lady, excels at formal and proper functions. Therefore it was not unusual that she was given the honor of manning the silver coffee server at a wedding reception, while Mrs. Cohen was in charge of the tea.
>
> Mother was thrilled until the next morning when she read the coverage in the Society section of the town's daily paper. It read: "The table was beautiful, and Mrs. Richter and Mrs. Cohen poured from both ends."
>
> —E.B.

Gambling is OK, but ladies do not shoot craps.

*

God gave you two eyes, two ears and one mouth. So you should watch and listen twice as much as you talk.

*

Your ancestors came over on the Mayflower, and I won't allow you to hitchhike to Florida.

*

When you put on the wedding dress, spit out the gum.

*

Things are always where you think they are, except when they're not.

*

Nothing will cool passion better than a sensible pair of knickers.

When unexpected company comes, throw everything in the bathtub, pull the shower curtain and pray nobody looks.

*

Your grandmother told me that whatever you do, wherever you go, you'll always find someone better than you, prettier than you, and smarter than you, so just be yourself. But it never happened to me.

*

A lady spends an hour after lunch in a straightback chair doing needlework.

*

Your father would never come to visit if he knew that you had roaches.

*

A little padding. It will be our secret.

*

Better you and your face should be shining than your floors.

*

Wear white at night, and if you aren't wearing any clothes, wave a hankie.

*

Don't let that compliment go to your head. Yes, you are pretty . . . pretty awful and pretty apt to stay that way.

*

You must learn to be assertive, but not with me.

*

Buy quality . . . on sale if possible.

*

You must learn good manners in case you get invited to the White House.

Do not wear patent leather shoes, because boys can see up your dress.

Two things are necessary when you buy a skirt: you have to be able to sit down, and you have to be able to breathe.

*

Always wear bangs, because without them you look too intelligent to ever catch a man.

My friend's mother grew up in a small Mississippi town with all the Southern hospitality and etiquette of a more mannered era. One summer she had a chance to visit some relatives in the North. With much anticipation, she took the train to New York and finally a subway to the Bronx. When she got there, she was starving and stopped at the first fruit vendor she saw. "Pardon me," she drawled. "Please, do you have any seedless grapes?"

The lines in the vendor's face tightened. He grabbed a cluster of grapes and shook them in her face. "So what's the matter, lady?" he barked. "You can't spit out?"

—L.A.

Wash your underwear by hand. It teaches you responsibility.

*

Don't walk over grates in the sidewalk. You never know who's down there.

My folks arrived late at a church supper at the same time as two other couples, much older than they and complete strangers to them. All the tables were taken, so a makeshift arrangement was made — two tables pulled together to accommodate the six of them. Mom sat at the juncture, wedged in between the tables. No one was too friendly. They were eating in stony silence, when my considerate father leaned over and inquired loudly, "Baby, do you feel all right between the legs?"

—L.A.

School And
Work

:10

Let The Fame Go And
Take The Cash

My daughter's kindergarten teacher had asked, "What does your mommy do?" and collected verbatim statements and illustrations from each child. My favorite was a picture of a big van with the caption, "My mommy drives carpool all day." Unfortunately for that mother, it was true.

But when I came to Eve's page, I was pleased with her concept of my situation: "My mommy is a librarian. Now she stays home and takes care of my brother and me." My eleven-year-old son, Ken, however, had an entirely different perspective.

"You're not a librarian."

"Yes, I am."

"But you haven't worked in eleven years."

"But that is my profession, and I'm still a librarian whether I'm working right now or not."

He gave this some thought before retorting, "But you're *dormant.*"

We are what we seem to be, and possibly more.

—L.A.

*

Go on and try it. The worst thing you can do is make a fool of yourself in front of all your friends.

*

Everybody is somebody, but some of us are bigger somebodies than others.

*

On your way up the ladder of success, watch out for the person behind you.

*

Use the grit in your gizzard!

*

You know what your problem is? You read too much.

*

You're smart. And you're a terrific typist. And you're well organized and efficient. You'd make a super secretary. Shhh, don't tell anybody.

*

What you haven't got in your head, you've got to have in your feet.

*

God gave you hips so you can tote groceries, carry children and hold up the pants if you have to.

Esther and I are used to working in unusual places. Thus when ideas come to us we can write anywhere. Once when I had gotten a brainstorm in a grocery store, we sat down in an empty shelf to jot it down. And on another occasion Esther accompanied me to my gynecologist appointment, taking notes all the way. She would have followed me into my examining room, but the doctor had only one table.

One day Esther and I had an important appointment at a downtown hotel, and we both wanted to be punctual. We carefully calculated how long it would take to maneuver through rush hour traffic, locate the building and find a parking garage. The next morning we sallied forth allowing forty-five minutes to get there.

Fifteen minutes later we were standing in the lobby. With a half-hour of unexpected work time, we looked in vain for two empty chairs. We finally found them in the ladies room. That we were sitting in the chairs under the towel dispenser didn't phase us at all. Engrossed in our work, we paid no attention to the comings and goings until we became aware of an elegantly dressed woman standing in front of us with dripping hands and a crying baby in her arms.

Esther thoughtfully handed her a towel. "Oh, thank you," she said, giving me the baby to hold. She dried her hands and retrieved her child. We resumed our work, only to be interrupted by a flash of metal and the tinkling of coins. With a flourish, the woman tossed two quarters in an ashtray and left.

Incredulously I asked Esther, "Do you suppose Louisa May Alcott got her start this way?"

"I don't think so," she replied, "but if we stay long enough, maybe it will pay for the parking!"

—L.A.

If your professor is brilliant but can't teach, find a dumber one who can.

*

Invest in land...it's the salt of the earth.

*

When I sent you to school to major in education, I didn't mean sex education.

*

I've been on the wrong side of the desk all these years. You'd better be on the other side.

*

Never learn how to iron. If you do, someone will expect you to do it.

*

If you are old enough to teach school, you're old enough to get out of bed the first time I call you.

*

It ain't braggin' if you can do it.

*

It's good to know a little about everything, except for some things when it's better not to know anything at all.

*

Women today are expected to know everything and show everything. That's a good way to blow everything.

*

Good Karma won't get you in *Who's Who*.

*

Your boss may be tough, but she'll never ask you to sit on her lap.

Don't pour coffee and don't take notes.

If you want to make an A in college, never sit farther back than the second row.

*

Your guru may know the meaning of life, but he can't help you pass physics.

*

Why do you look so bedraggled after a day's work, and the cleaning lady still looks neat?

*

Don't be afraid to deal with important people. Remember, they once filled their diapers, too.

*

When people discuss their accomplishments at a convention, the amount you should believe is proportional to their distance from the bar.

*

You haven't got a chance getting that job. Of course, Columbus's mother probably said the same thing before he went to see Isabella.

*

A nurse is caught between the doctor's invincibility and the patient's vulnerability.

*

In nursing school, they tell you Florence Nightingale was the lady with the lamp. They failed to mention that she held a bedpan in the other hand.

*

When are you going to stop writing songs and get a real job?

*

A good stockbroker is more important than a good hairdresser.

A Phi Beta Kappa key won't unlock any doors, but it will grease the hinges.

*

If you go through life trading on your good looks, there'll come a time when no one wants to trade.

A reporter doing a story on our book felt that a picture of us working at McDonald's would be a unique angle since we did much of our writing there.

We returned to McDonald's the day after the article was published. I arrived first and ordered two cups of coffee. Heading for our table, I lugged my coat and briefcase with one hand and balanced my purse and tray precariously in the other. A tug at my elbow interrupted this juggling act, and a ten-year-old girl giggled out a request for an autograph.

Lynne arrived and we shared the satisfaction of having our first fan. Shortly thereafter two elderly ladies approached our table. They stopped, pointed and finally mustered the courage to speak. They told us that they recognized us from our picture and were very enthusiastic about the book. Naturally, we were flattered.

When they left, we resumed our work. I was engrossed in our writing until I noticed that an attractive man at the next table was trying to get my attention. He finally cleared his throat and said, "Excuse me."

I puffed up ready for the compliment and in my most sophisticated voice murmured, "Yes?"

He leaned over, gazed into my eyes, and asked, "Is it always this cold in here?"

So much for fleeting fame.

—E.B.

A friend's daughter went to medical school and was invited to join the medical fraternity. When her mother heard the news, she replied, "Now you'll be your father's fraternity brother!"

✻

We didn't spend $12,000 for you to hang your diploma in the laundry room.

✻

Don't play the trumpet, you'll get fat lips.

✻

You can't take a career to bed with you.

✻

When a woman goes back to work full time, the first thing to go is friends, and the second thing to go is sex.

✻

Forget the Gucci bag. The first thing to get when you become an executive is an accountant.

✻

If you're going on a business trip with your boss, make sure he knows you mean business.

Mother and a friend decided to audit a course in the stock market at Rice University. They phoned Professor Hodges, the class instructor, who most willingly gave his permission. But since that course was only offered in the spring, he suggested that they attend his fall course in statistics. They registered and gamely appeared at the assigned classroom.

Mother and her friend bought the textbook, studied the lessons and continued to find the course fascinating. They were encouraged that statistics was not the difficult subject my father had warned them about. This went on for several months.

One day the professor announced there would be no class because his wife was having a baby. Before the next class resumed, Mother asked another student whether Dr. Hodges's wife had had a boy or girl.

"Who are you talking about?" he replied.

"Dr. Hodges, the professor."

"The professor's name is Mackey," he informed her.

Turning to her friend, Mother said, "If the professor's name is Mackey, who do you suppose he thinks *we* are?"

After class they searched for an office with the name Hodges on it. Entering, they asked the gentleman at the desk, "Are you Dr. Hodges?"

"Yes," he acknowledged.

"We're the two ladies who called you about auditing your course in statistics."

"Where have you been? I was disappointed that you didn't come."

"No one told us that Mr. Mackey was giving the course, and we've been sitting in his class all semester," Mother explained.

"Young ladies, are you under the impression that you are taking a course in statistics?"

Taken aback, Mother admitted that was just what they thought. Roaring with laughter, he said, "Be careful how you use your newly acquired knowledge. The course you've been taking is Income Tax Accounting!"

—L.A.

There's more to business than the tricks of the trade.

*

Having a partner means twice the problems, twice the aggravation and half the money.

*

A credit card is nothing but a plastic coated mugger.

*

When you win the Nobel Prize, it won't matter that you didn't pass the President's Physical Fitness Test.

*

How can anyone flunk sex education?

*

As a woman, the only thing you're in control of is what you're sitting on.

*

Never own more stores than you have relatives to run them.

*

If you want to get a good job, keep your foot on the sidewalk and out of your mouth.

*

When it comes to taking care of a house, your dad is not a chauvinist; he just doesn't do that kind of work.

*

If you can't dress for success, at least dress for trying.

*

If you want to take up sewing, better you should become a surgeon.

Guilt

11

Why Should I Be Reasonable? I'm Your Mother

I was halfway through a two-week visit from my in-laws. I cherish them very much but was suffering from a privacy deprivation. I had not yet mastered the art of leaving them alone in the house without feeling guilty, and my in-laws don't particularly enjoy going out. My tolerance level is only three days.

On the eighth day my husband finally suggested that Dad take Mom to Callaway Gardens, which is about an hour and a half's drive southwest of Atlanta, to see the flowers in bloom. "Where is that?" Dad asked.

"Oh, it's a great place. There's a greenhouse full of tropical plants, thousands of acres of flowering trails and guided tours. You know how Mom loves flowers."

"How far is it?" Dad repeated more firmly.

"Uh, about ninety miles, but it's gorgeous and you'll have a great time."

"*Ninety miles* just to see some flowers? Are you crazy?"

All this time Mom was silently doing her needlepoint. As the argument got louder and louder, Mom finally interrupted. "Lynne, dear, don't worry. We didn't come here to have a good time; we just came to visit you."

—L.A.

*

You should only have a child like you.

*

You can do anything you want to with a boy, but I'll be sitting on your shoulder and you won't enjoy it.

*

A mother always knows.

*

Your father and I would do anything to make you happy, but you're asking too much.

*

I just hope I live long enough to be a burden to you.

*

Pregnant with a third child, and the other two are not out of diapers yet. How could you do this to me?

*

When you grow up, I hope you have a child just like you, and that will be punishment enough.

> Knowing that her old-fashioned mother did not take well to surprises, Teresa dreaded phoning her bad news so soon after the wedding. When she finally found the courage to call, she told her mother about her annulment. The news was greeted by a long silence. Her mother's only comment before hanging up was, "Dear, are you going to write the thank-you notes?"
>
> —L.A.

All my life I've sacrificed for you. Now you're ready to throw me into a volcano.

❉

I keep waiting by the phone for that special ring that tells me you are pregnant.

❉

Don't worry, there's someone for everyone…even you.

❉

If we don't catch you, God will.

❉

God bless guilt. It made you what you are today.

❉

I never demand anything of my children. I always make the best of everything.

❉

I'm not complaining, I'm just surprised.

❉

I never make plans for my children, but if you don't do it you'll be sorry.

❉

I made you what you are today. I hope you're satisfied.

All day long I stand over a hot stove and what do I get? Grief and aggravation.

*

Set a good example for your younger sister. Remember, when you do something wrong, you are doing it for two.

*

For a girl who is supposed to be so smart, you sure do some stupid things.

*

If you don't want to break my heart, you will stay a virgin and happy.

I never fully understood the meaning of the word *cad* until I met my best friend's steady. While professing his everlasting affection for her, he expanded his horizons with every available girl. My friend and her family seemed oblivious to his escapades. Lacking the heart to shatter her illusions, I watched silently as she ran his errands, did his laundry and cleaned his apartment. Her mother served him delicious meals and knitted him sweaters.

One day he brought some trousers for her mother to fix for a camping trip with his brother. Actually, I knew that he was really taking his latest conquest. I could bear it no longer. As soon as he left, I went into a tirade about how much he took advantage of her. "How can you date a man who treats you so badly?"

When I finally wound down she calmly said, "Don't be so upset. I realized what was happening, and I'm not going to see him anymore. But I know that he'll always remember me."

I said, "Well, I certainly hope he will be sorry."

"Oh, he will," she replied, "especially when he can't get his pants off tonight. Mother jammed his zipper."

—E.B.

When a woman your age buys a cat, that ends my hope for grandchildren.

I thank God that my other children don't treat me the way you do.

✻

You'll forget. I'll forget. You'll forget. But I'll remember, and don't you forget it.

✻

What can you tell a psychiatrist that you can't tell your own mother?

✻

I may not always be right, but I have never been wrong.

✻

My daughter. A college girl. Listen to her big mouth. That's why she went to college—to talk to me like that.

✻

I can always move in with my daughter . . . God forbid!

✻

You don't have to invite me to your party. I'll just come and help in the kitchen.

✻

Fine. It's your life. If you want to ruin it, it's OK with me.

✻

If you dream about boys, it's your subconscious feelings trying to get out. Stop it!

✻

Don't do anything wrong. You'll look different and people will know.

✻

I never thought you'd turn out this good.

✻

Mothers are supposed to worry.

> Some mothers nag their daughters constantly about their weight; others are forthright in their attack. But with my mother, who always wants to spare anyone's feelings, her criticism takes the long way around.
>
> The moment she arrives for a visit, Mother will invariably tell me how good I look, regardless of chubby cheeks and the settling sands of time. I never believe her because she compliments everyone, but I never give it much thought either. Until a recent visit.
>
> She stepped off the plane, took one look, and exclaimed for the whole airport to hear, "Oh, Lynne, you look so much *better!*"
>
> —L.A.

A letter once a week is not asking too much.

*

If you can afford the long-distance calls, you can afford a weekend with your mother.

*

I never left *you* with a babysitter.

*

Now that you can cook and drive, you won't need me anymore.

Children's Sayings

12

Don't Tap Dance On The Toilet

In these space-probing, freeze-dried, high-tech times, Mother frantically sends messages to her little girl, hoping her modern advice will not only shine through all the garbage but be superior to what her own mother told her twenty-five or thirty years ago.

However... what goes out of Mother's mouth often seems to have been scrambled by some mysterious computer by the time it enters Daughter's ears and appears once more on her lips. After garnering quotes from hundreds of girl scouts and little girls in nursery schools and kindergartens, we discovered this slightly altered information is often saner and always more delightful than what Mother originally said.

But before reading this chapter of advice young girls interpreted from Mama, here is the true story of a little girl who lived many years ago—one we think puts everything into perspective and helps get a good handle (so to speak) on reality.

The scene opens with the little girl visiting her grandparents on the family farm. Grandmother thought the child would learn about nature by watching the farm hands milk the cows, so she sent her out to the barn. But she was taken aback when the child returned only a few moments later looking very unhappy.

"Well," asked the grandmother, "what did you think of that?"

"I thought it was sad," answered the little girl.

"What do you mean?" responded the grandmother, quite surprised.

"I thought it was sad," insisted the child. "How would you like it if somebody pulled on your roots like that?"

So, mothers: Before you send your six-year-old out to meet the world armed with your sage advice, perhaps it would be helpful to hear what she will *really* be taking with her. Here it is—straight, honest, just the way we heard it....

❊

Don't tell your friend where babies come from. Her mama may be keeping it as a surprise.

❊

Never open a President before your birthday.

❊

I'll put a band-aid on your pinky-toe, but I won't kiss it.

❊

When you get married, you need flowers, a priest, wine, music, doughnuts and a husband.

❊

To fry an egg, crack it on the sink and put it in the bowl before it slides down the drain.

OK, Motormouth. Time to turn off the switch.

*

Apples are for biting. Friends are not.

*

You bumped your chin because you are growing up. Last year it was your forehead.

*

If you can hear the ice cream truck a block away, you can come in the first time I call you.

*

You don't have to close your eyes, you just have to go to sleep.

*

Mary Lou Retton does not suck her thumb on the balance beam.

*

Go play. You're helping me too much.

Aunt DeVera took her daughter to the circus. They sat in the very front row, where the child was entranced. As she watched the procession of animals and performers, she ate popcorn, cotton candy, hotdogs and other assorted goodies.

All the food, excitement and circus smells were finally too much, and she told her mother that she felt ill. "Wait," my aunt told her. "Throw up when the elephants pass by and no one will notice." So she did. The elephants got the blame, and it was all shoveled away in the end.

—E.B.

Changing the TV channel when Daddy is watching a ballgame is very dangerous.

*

Don't tap dance on the toilet.

*

If you hang upside down all day, the blood will rush to your head and your feet will get lonely.

*

Nice girls don't spit.

*

You have to go, but you don't have to have any fun.

*

You can't go to the bathroom standing up because you will get your feet wet.

*

Saying "I'm sorry" in a very nice voice is not enough. You also have to stop pulling his nose.

*

You can read any book in the house that you can reach.

*

Wash behind your ears; you never know who's going to look back there.

*

Don't kick your brother's school lunch. A smooshed lunch is not a delicious lunch.

*

Take the puppy outside when he has to go. Do not dump him in the toilet.

Don't stick your finger in an electric sock.

After you wet the bed, you should have changed your pajamas before you crawled in bed with Daddy.

*

It wasn't nice to put peanut butter down your brother's trumpet.

*

You're on a diet because spaghetti is not a good vegetable.

*

A baby sister is nicer than a goat. You'll get used to her.

*

Daddy's vasectomy is interesting, but I don't think the teacher will want you to bring him to school for Show and Tell.

*

You are getting new shoes because your old shoes are giving your feet a headache.

*

You aren't old enough to wear makeup, so put it where people cannot see it.

*

Be nice a week before you ask Daddy for money.

*

I know you licked the plate clean, but I still have to put it in the dishwasher.

*

You can invite the President to dinner if you ask his mother first.

*

You are going to sit there until you finish your peas, even if you become a little old lady with two peas to go.

Belching the entire alphabet is not an accomplishment.

*

Brother can't breathe when you sit on his face.

One day I overheard two four-year-old girls bickering. It soon degenerated into a game of one-upmanship. "My mommy's nicer than your mommy."

"Well, my mommy's prettier than your mommy."

"But my mommy's smarter than your mommy."

"Oh yeah? Well, my daddy's bigger than your daddy."

"Well, my daddy's gonna beat your daddy's brains out."

With hands on her hips, the second girl drew herself up to her full three feet and concluded victoriously: "Well, ha, ha, ha. My daddy ain't *got* no brains!"

—L.A.

Celebrity Quotes

13

Lydia E. Pinkham And Other Famous Women

A friend of mine doesn't like liquor. It isn't a matter of conviction, she simply doesn't like the taste. When she was a young woman, she was invited to a cabaret by the handsomest, most eligible man in town. Her mother advised that since she wanted to look sophisticated but didn't want to drink, she should order a "Shirley Temple."

My friend and her date arrived at the club and joined several other couples. The waiter came to the table, and each person gave a drink order. "Please, I'll have a Brandy Alexander." "I'll have a Dempsey cocktail." "A Pink Lady, please." "Jack Daniels." "A Tom Collins." "Bring me a Rob Roy." By the time the waiter got to her, all she could think of was, "A Lydia Pinkham, please...on the rocks."

Whether it's Lydia Pinkham or Shirley Temple, we've found that most women — famous or not — have a great deal in common when it comes to what Mama told them.

By their gracious sharing of remembered words of wisdom, the prominent women in this chapter allow us to touch them in a special and personal way. Their talent sets them apart, but their candor makes them a part of us all. And for this, we thank them.

Many of the quotes are revealing (about mother and daughter), some show that Mama's advice was indeed taken (as with Helen Gurley Brown and Shana Alexander), but most show that they simply had mothers like the rest of us, women who — wise or not — took the term "Mother" very seriously. Here, then, are our thirty famous women, who, when Mama spoke, apparently listened. . . .

—E.B.

*

Helen Gurley Brown: Author, Editor of *Cosmopolitan*
My mother told me from the moment I could comprehend words that "(a) a girl shouldn't marry too early, (b) she should use her brain and (c) she shouldn't rush to have children." During a period when everyone said the only thing that mattered was grabbing a husband and being fecund, she realized how lovely it was to have a brain and not only make use of it, but get paid for the usage.

*

Julia Child: Chef, Author, Television Personality
"You're tall, so they're going to look at you. Stand up straight, then, and give them something to look at."

*

Shirley Booth: Actress
"What you are speaks so much louder than what you say that I can't hear a word you're saying."

Loretta Lynn: Country Music Singer
"We may be poor, but there is no excuse for filth, because the water is free and soap doesn't cost that much."

✳

Contessa De Brusset of Austria
Grandmother, Princess Czaki, took my daughter Robbie to lunch at the Hotel Meurice in Paris. A couple came in and spoke to them, but Grandmother ignored them. After they moved on, Robbie said, "Grandmother, that couple spoke to you. Aren't you going to acknowledge them?" "Dear, they've been trying for three generations to break into society. We ignore them — their grandfather was in the trades."

✳

Phyllis Diller: Comedienne
My mother had a quote for everything:
> "Don't go off half-cocked."
> "Laughter is the best medicine."
> "We grow old too soon and smart too late."

✳

Agnes de Mille: Choreographer
I never knew my grandmother, Mrs. Henry George, but she must have been marvelous. She said to my mother: "Never destroy any aspect of a living organism, because what you take to be the wild branch may be the heart of the tree."

✳

Roberta Flack: Vocalist
"God don't like ugly."

Betty White: Actress
My mother is dynamite and has given me lots of goodies to live by through the years. The most useful to me was, "Don't ever try to fool that face in the mirror. Be sure you can always look yourself right in the eye."

*

Phoebe Snow: Vocalist, Musician, Composer
"Don't pick it (whatever), it won't heal."
"Always wait for a boy to call you."
"Hard-boiled eggs give you beautiful hair and a beautiful singing voice."
She was the kind of mother who tirelessly tried to convince me that if I ate a healthy meal of chicken and green salad, my life would probably improve one hundred percent.

*

Minnie Pearl: Comedienne
"Never trust a man who writes *too* beautiful a love letter. He's had too much practice."
"Never follow the dress of others because it is 'the style.' You are an individual; create your own style."

*

Lee Meriwether: Actress, Former Miss America
"Just remember, when you are pointing your finger at someone, there are three pointing back at you!"

*

Joyce D. Miller: Past President, Coalition of Labor Union Women
"If you plant peaches in children, you get peaches.... If you plant potatoes, you'll get potatoes."

Things always happened to my mother. Thus, when we began working on this chapter, I asked her if she recalled any incidents involving celebrities. A week later, her letter arrived. "Dear Lynne," it began. "I've thought and thought but can't recall any experiences with movie stars other than connecting Dale Evans's phone at the phone company, unless you count having breakfast in Las Vegas at a table adjoining Sally Kellerman and Walter Matthau and eavesdropping on their conversation about the hardships of growing up in Hell's Kitchen, or overhearing Joan Fontaine at the Los Angeles airport saying that she was in mortal dread of flying or having Gene Tierney say, 'Thank you, these packages are so heavy' when I held the door open for her at the post office. Of course there was the time when I was eight and a half months pregnant and Tyrone Power almost had to deliver *you*. But I'm sure that nobody would be interested in that story."

—L.A.

Shana Alexander: Journalist
My mother always told me to "figure it out for yourself." Eventually I did.

*

Edith Head: Fashion Designer
I remember two bits of advice Mother gave me. The first, so that one wouldn't forget, was, "Always write it down." And the other was to always be sure that your hair was neat, because people would judge you by the way you looked.

*

Edie Adams: Singer, Actress
"Sing a pretty song and wear a pretty dress."

Madeline Kahn: Actress, Comedienne
"Sing — don't cry."
"Success is no accident."
"Love is everywhere but hard to find."

✳

Glenda Jackson: Actress
My mother always urged me to be sure I had a clean handkerchief and clean knickers in case I was knocked down in the road.

✳

Margaret Chase Smith: United States Senator (retired)
"Obey the Golden Rule — live by it!"
"Always be a lady, even when you are firm and assert yourself."
"Anything that is worth doing is worth doing right the first time."

✳

Butterfly McQueen: Actress
My grandmother said, "If there's a rock in the road and you need to move it, if you can't move it by yourself, leave it there." In other words, be independent.

✳

Arlene Dahl: Actress, Business Executive
"You're never fully dressed unless you're wearing a smile."

✳

Sylvia Porter: Journalist, Author, Economics Specialist
From the time I was in my cradle, I can remember my mother saying: "You will have the career that I missed by marrying and having babies immediately. You will have the life that I forfeited because I did not realize that I was a person as well as a woman." It is the key explanation of why I am what I am.

If a prominent woman visits a city like New York or Washington, she usually merits some publicity and a crowd. But that's nothing compared to the reception offered this same famous person in a small town. The crowd is usually the entire village, and the town's newspaper will publish anything the celebrity says or does.

When Eleanor Roosevelt came to speak, my Indiana town was no exception. I was especially thrilled because she was going to lecture from my father's pulpit, and the entire community was invited. Naturally, she was offered the use of my father's office.

After Mrs. Roosevelt left, it took several days for the town to settle down. One day Mother went to Dad's office to pick up his mail. When she came home she said, "You'll never believe what I just saw." When I asked her to elaborate, she explained.

"I entered your father's office and heard voices coming from his bathroom. I opened the door with some hesitation, and you'll never guess what I found. It was Miss Hinkel's Brownie Troop." "The whole troop?" I gasped. "What were they doing in Dad's bathroom?" "Well," Mother replied, "Miss Hinkel was showing them the actual place where Eleanor Roosevelt had sat."

—E.B.

Liz Carpenter: Author, Former Press Secretary to Mrs. Lyndon B. Johnson
My Grandmothers Robertson and Sutherland were women of deep family loyalty and the pride of the Scots. "Remember who you are" was a frequent admonition to behave yourself — behave like your forefathers would expect. "Make something of yourself" was my mother's request, and I shall always remember she believed I could.

Dale Evans Rogers: Actress, Vocalist, Author

My mother, Bettie Sue Smith, was a terrific inspiration in my life. She was a devout Christian but extremely practical about rules for living. When she was eighty-six, she cautioned me about too much traveling and speaking. I would say, "Lord will fit the back to the burden," and she would reply, "Lord also gave you a head with common sense; why don't you use it?"

＊

Maya Angelou: Author

My mother is wise and funny a lovely combination. She advised me, "Don't allow anyone to make you over. Just say, 'My mother raised me,' and remember you were grown when you left home."

＊

Helen Hayes: Actress

My mother liked a saying of vaudevillians in the old days: "Always leave them wanting more." I've applied that to acting, to writing, to speeches — just about every facet of my life in public.

＊

Celestine Sibley: Author, Newspaper Columnist

The kind of wisdom which came my way was pretty pragmatic and very dated, I am afraid. Little girls lifted the backs of their skirts when they sat down but were careful to pull down the front of their skirts. You looked the other way when you passed a pool room, never used public toilets and never asked questions of strangers, unless they wore brass buttons of policemen, firemen or railroad conductors, or a Masonic emblem. And finally, not terribly original but oddly sustaining, that you can do anything you have to do.

Joan Rivers: Comedienne, Author

"When you pick a friend, pick her ugly so you'll always look good."

"Make sure the man you marry is more in love with you than you are with him, so he'll have the sleepless nights while you get your beauty rest."

*

Judy Woodruff: Television Newswoman

The one thing that came immediately to mind was, "Pretty is as pretty does." There were numerous other admonitions about not starting things I couldn't finish, about always striving to do the best I could, about being polite to other people. And, my father always telling me to, "Do what your mother says."

*

Elaine de Kooning: Artist

"Always take care of the luxuries, dear, the necessities will take care of themselves."

LYNNE ALPERN and ESTHER BLUMENFELD conduct workshops on humor and their articles have been published in numerous national publications. They've written material for some of the country's leading comedians, and they're the authors of the book, *The Smile Connection: How To Use Humor in Dealing With People.*